Storm Group

A Study Guide for *Show Yourself a Man*

BRAD LARSON

LUCIDBOOKS

Storm Group
A Study Guide for Show Yourself a Man
End the confusion. Form your identity. Forge your manhood.
Copyright © 2017 by Brad Larson

Published by Lucid Books in Houston, TX.
www.LucidBooksPublishing.com

ISBN 10: 163296130X
ISBN 13: 9781632961303

Special Sales: Most Lucid Books titles are available in special quantity discounts. Custom imprinting or excerpting can also be done to fit special needs. Contact Lucid Books at Info@LucidBooksPublishing.com.

Table of Contents

What Is a Storm Group?

Martin Luther's dad wanted him to become a lawyer. Luther's dad was a miner and had learned the brutal lessons of manual labor in a mine: the injuries, the dust, the dangers. He wanted his boy to choose a better way to make a living, so he sent Martin to school in Germany. Martin followed his father's plan.

That is, until the storm.

One day, Martin was caught in a terrifying storm. The ground beneath him trembled as lightning descended like javelins thrown from heaven. In a fit of desperation, he called out for help. His dad had probably taught him about the patron saint of miners, St. Anne. Martin blurted out a plea to St. Anne and promised to become a monk if she saved him. The storm subsided, and Luther was set on a new path. This new path would not lead him to a law office, though. This new path would lead him to start the Protestant Reformation.

Now, I don't believe in praying to saints. Don't get distracted there. God calmed that storm, not St. Anne. I want us to focus on the profound effect of the storm. It was scary. It was disruptive. It changed Luther's life. And it set Luther on a path of an adventurous life with Jesus.

That is why we call these Storm Groups.

This group you are starting is not a casual coffee group. It can be that, of course, but if you take it seriously it will be a storm that changes your life.

Make no mistake: you will encounter spiritual opposition in this group. When you move toward Jesus, darkness advances upon you. Satan hates advancement toward Jesus. You are a man, a warrior with great potential to do damage to the enemy—and the enemy will not spare you as you gather strength in your Storm Group. Your group will become inconvenient, messy, or boring. You won't want to show up. But you must push through. You must fight for your group.

If you follow the plan laid out in this guide, God will create a storm of life change. It might be scary, but it'll be fun—and it'll be worth it. You will grow closer to the Lord, and in doing so you will grow in your wisdom as a man and you'll have some brothers around you for support and strength.

GROUND RULES

Small groups are always hard, but discipline and parameters help keep the group on track.

Let's set some ground rules:

1. *Show up on time.* If you are on time, you show respect for the group. Start on time whether everyone is there or not. End at a specified time. Your hard start and stop will help get your group in the game.

2. *Be open.* It may take some time for your group to open up about their lives, and that's okay. But don't bother joining a Storm Group if you're going to hide your secret sins, questions, and fears. You need to share your life with your group so you can apply God's grace and wisdom to it.

3. *Keep secrets.* Unless your group member confesses a serious crime, your group needs to operate with confidence. It's like attorney-client privilege. What happens in the group, stays in the group.

4. *Read the material.* You will be asked to read one chapter of *Show Yourself a Man* per week. Make sure you read so you can contribute to the group. (If you can't make the group meeting, go ahead and read the chapter so you stay in sync with the group.)

5. *Have fun. Enjoy yourself!* Don't take yourself too seriously. This group will be heavy, but it should be fun.

THE FORMAT

This guide will walk you through the content of *Show Yourself a Man* one chapter at a time. You will be responsible to read the assigned chapter before each meeting. During each meeting you will talk through the questions in this guide.

You'll need a leader. He does not need to be a preacher, scholar, or black belt. He just needs to be a guy who loves Jesus and is willing to be consistent in getting everyone together. He must be willing to facilitate dialogue among men. He will round everyone up and keep everyone accountable for being there.

THE FOLLOW-UP

Storm Groups meet for a defined period of time. They are not designed to go on forever, although it is understood that some permanently formed men's groups may use the Storm Group content for a focused study. That's certainly okay. (It is a good thing if your *Show Yourself a Man* Storm Group creates a men's group that continues meeting on a permanent basis—you'll just need some new content after you finish with the Storm Group Guide.)

Given that most groups will be short—only 12 weeks—it is imperative that the group doesn't completely disband afterward.

The leader of each group must agree to follow up with the group via email one year after the last meeting. Each man will use the Checking In content at the back of this guide to assess how he is doing. He will then scan his results and send to the group for counsel and encouragement. It is best if the group can meet again to discuss their results, but the leader must do what he can do to assemble the group—even if it's just a digital meeting. After the one-year follow-up, the group may disband. (It is encouraged that the group stay in touch, however.)

Okay. Let's do this.

CHAPTER 1

Aimless Male Bipeds

FLY-BY OVERVIEW

Men, we are in trouble. We're falling behind. We are more incarcerated and less educated. Our postmodern world is an odd place for a full-hearted man to live. We no longer need to grab a bow and head to the woods to kill our dinner—we can just order a pizza with a few clicks. We live in relative peace, so most of us don't have to fight. To what end do we apply our strength? Have we been outsourced? To be a man in today's world, one must struggle with relativism, technology, and a confused cultural narrative.

GROUP DISCUSSION QUESTIONS

1. Have you noticed the cultural confusion around manhood? What have you observed?

------

2. Have you delayed growing up? If so, how?

3. When you have been given responsibility, how did it change you? What did you learn?

4. How might our struggles as men highlight our need for Jesus?

PRAYER

Have one man volunteer to pray over the topic of male aimlessness. Have him pray for the group and ask for direction from God. You can use the following prayer if it's helpful:

> *Father, we desperately need you. We confess as men in today's world, we struggle. We are sometimes confused. But you are not a God of confusion. You are a God of clarity, strength, and purpose. We long for the presence of Jesus in our lives as men. So we ask that the Spirit would illuminate our need for Jesus and that we would draw near to him. In Jesus's name, amen.*

TAKE ACTION

Pay attention to the culture around you. What does it say about men? Take notice this week of the cultural narrative around manhood.

CHAPTER 2

Growing Up

FLY-BY OVERVIEW

Growing up is hard. Our childhood shapes us and molds us into the men we are today. Each stage of growing up has its own joys and challenges, from boyhood to adolescence to The Precipice. The world shapes us over time, but if we become intentional men, we will, conversely, shape the world over time. With God's help, that is. We need to unearth our past so we can build our future.

GROUP DISCUSSION QUESTIONS

1. How was your childhood?

2. What good or bad masculine examples did you have in your life when you were young? How did they affect you?

3. Are there young men and boys in your life who see you as their example? What are you showing them?

_____

_____

_____

_____

_____

4. What lessons might God have for you from your childhood?

_____

_____

_____

_____

_____

PRAYER

Have one man volunteer to pray over the topic of growing up. Have him pray for the group and ask for direction from God. You can use the following prayer if it's helpful:

> _Lord, it is not lost on us that our very breath is from you. So when you knit us together in our mother's womb, we know you had plans for us. Some of us have had hard childhoods, while others have been blessed to have good ones. Either way we know that all things work together for the good of those who love you. Lord, will you reveal to us what lessons we might learn from our childhood? Will you help us shape the younger men in our lives as you shape us? We submit to your will, God. In Jesus's name, amen._

TAKE ACTION

Consider your upbringing. Consider the men who have gone before you, on whose shoulders you stand. Were they godly men? Were they godless men? Who were they at heart? Think about how these men have shaped you: your values, your attributes, and your virtues.

CHAPTER 3

Idol Machines

FLY-BY OVERVIEW

The real world can be tough. When a young man enters the real world, it's fun and new—at least for a little while. Once the novelty of our freedom wears off, we start to look for new objects to distract or entertain us. We search for meaning. We pursue idols—false gods— and worship them. It could be a hobby, money, sex, or our reputation. Idols can be inherently good or inherently sinful, but they are dangerous because they divert our worship away from God. We need to kill them.

"You shall not make idols for yourselves or erect an image or pillar, and you shall not set up a figured stone in your land to bow down to it, for I am the Lord your God" (Lev. 26:1).

GROUP DISCUSSION QUESTIONS

1. How have you made sex an idol? Do you have anything to confess to your brothers about this?

   _____

   _____

   _____

   _____

2. Have you ever made money an idol? If so, how?

_____

_____

_____

_____

3. Do you crave comfort? Why do you think that is?

_____

_____

_____

_____

4. What idols would you like to kill? How might killing them bring you closer to Jesus?

_____

_____

_____

_____

PRAYER

Have one man volunteer to pray over the topic of idolatry. Have him pray for the group and ask for direction from God. You can use the following prayer if it's helpful:

> *God, we must confess that we have pursued false gods. And when we have, we have found them lacking. Idols have no power, no salvation, and no peace. They only bring angst and heartache. We repent of our idolatry and trust you. Lead us away from the temptation to trust false gods and lead us toward you. That is what we want, God—but we are weak. We need help. In Jesus's name, amen.*

TAKE ACTION

Killing idols is not merely a mental and spiritual exercise. If, for example, you've made sex an idol and thus have a pornography problem, the damage from your idolatry extends beyond you. You will need to kill your idol by placing accountability in your life, and you may need to confess your sin to your wife or girlfriend. There are three steps here: 1) awareness and earnest repentance, 2) practical steps to slay the idol, and 3) confession and reparation to those you've harmed. If you have a deep-seated addiction to your idol, you should consider seeking the help of a biblical counselor to help you.

CHAPTER 4

Forming Identity

FLY-BY OVERVIEW

A lot of us have allowed culture to form our understanding of who a man is and what he should live for. This will not do for the man seeking Jesus. We must form our identity before we forge our manhood. In order to build our identity, we must first dethrone ourselves from the center of our world. We must consider who Jesus is, because this answer will determine the trajectory of our lives. Who do you say he is? It is also important to know who Jesus says you are. *This will change everything.*

GROUP DISCUSSION QUESTIONS

1. In what ways have you tried to build a false identity?

_____

_____

_____

_____

_____

2. Have you placed yourself at the center of your life? If so, how can you remove yourself and acknowledge God as your King?

_____

_____

_____

_____

_____

3. Who do you say Jesus is?

_____

_____

_____

_____

4. What do you think Jesus thinks of you? How does this affect the way you live?

_____

_____

_____

_____

_____

PRAYER

Have one man volunteer to pray over the topic of forging masculine identity. Have him pray for the group and ask for direction from God. You can use the following prayer if it's helpful:

> _Father, I trust you. I believe I am saved by the blood of Jesus, by his work for me on the cross. In loving anguish he delivered my soul. God, make me a man. Make me your man. I do not want to be my own man; I want to be your son. Father me. Teach me. Guide me. Direct me on the path to my true identity so that on the way I might find more of you. In the holy name of Jesus, amen._

TAKE ACTION

Get some time away this week. You don't need to go live in a van down by the river for a month; just get away for an hour somewhere quiet and serene. Take your Bible and a journal. Read Romans 8:12–17 and reflect on it in your own way. Think about your identity, who God says you are. Consider how this should cause you to live differently.

CHAPTER 5

Show Yourself a Man

FLY-BY OVERVIEW

King David's dying words to his son Solomon were, "Be strong, and show yourself a man" (1 Kings 2:2). These are nuclear words. David goes on to explain to Solomon what he means. Walk in God's ways, keep his commandments, follow after him. When God calls men, he doesn't choose the superheroes. He chooses the antiheroes—guys like you and me. He doesn't call complete men; he builds them. When we walk in his ways, delighting in Jesus, we grow closer to him. We see that living his way works. We see that his commandments are rooted in love. We need each other as we walk in his ways.

GROUP DISCUSSION QUESTIONS

1. How do David's dying words affect you?

----

2. What does it look like to walk in the ways of God?

_____

_____

_____

_____

_____

3. Why does it matter if we keep God's commandments? What happens when we don't?

_____

_____

_____

_____

_____

4. What is the difference between living for God and living with God?

_____

_____

_____

_____

_____

PRAYER

Have one man volunteer to pray for the group to show themselves as men. Have him pray for the group and ask for direction from God. You can use the following prayer if it's helpful:

> *Heavenly Father, we want to walk in your ways. We want to be strong and show ourselves as men. We know you created the world and that you know how everything works. We know you designed us to be fearless and faithful men. And, Lord, we confess we are inclined either to live without you or to try and earn your love. Neither works. We want to live with you. In Jesus's name, amen.*

TAKE ACTION

John Piper says, "God is most glorified in us when we are most satisfied in him." Walking in God's ways is not about keeping a set of rules, it is about the pursuit of joy in God. Some of us are inclined to live for God—that is, to try and earn his affection. Others try to live as if God exists but he is somewhere far, far away. Neither is a wise path for living.

The key is joy.

The longings of our hearts are satisfied in full through Jesus. When we delight in him, in his finished work on the cross, in the Spirit's power to move in our lives—we become more joyful.

This week take some time to enjoy the Lord. What does that look like for you? A walk in nature? Quiet prayer alone in your room? Worship music? Maybe it's fishing or taking a long run. Are you alone or with some brothers? Do your thing in your own way, but schedule some time to grow your joy in the Lord.

CHAPTER 6

Open Your Mind

FLY-BY OVERVIEW

Learning is a crucial part of manhood, but too many of us have given up our pursuit of wisdom. Many of us haven't read much since high school and we lean too much on Google. Aliteracy (being able to read but not being interested in doing so) is on the rise in our society. We must cultivate our minds if we want to cultivate virtue. Jesus was a voracious learner. Learning helps us frame what we see in the world. It rounds us out and sharpens us at the same time. But it takes time, which is counterintuitive in our fast-paced society. Knowledge is about massaging worship of God into the heart, not puffing up the brain.

GROUP DISCUSSION QUESTIONS

1. Do you consider yourself a curious learner? Why or why not?

_____

_____

_____

_____

_____

2. What book, other than *Show Yourself a Man*, will you commit to reading? (The group will hold you accountable.)

_____

_____

_____

_____

3. How do you filter what you learn to make sure you're taking in truth and not lies?

_____

_____

_____

_____

4. What do you think made Jesus so curious?

_____

_____

_____

_____

PRAYER

Have one man volunteer to pray over the topic of seeking wisdom. Have him pray for the group and ask for direction from God. You can use the following prayer if it's helpful:

> *God, we seek wisdom. And we know that wisdom is found in you alone. You are the owner of all truth. As we seek to learn, we ask that the Spirit would make our hearts burn in worship. When we learn more about the world, we see your majesty. Show us more, God. Show us more. And as you do, please keep us humble. Help us be wise for your sake and for the good of others. In Jesus's name, amen.*

TAKE ACTION

In the questions above, you committed to reading a certain book. Buy that book this week.

CHAPTER 7

Forge Your Vessel

FLY-BY OVERVIEW

Our bodies are our vessel for the journey of life. God grants us our earthly bodies as a gift, so we must be good stewards of them. Regardless of whether or not we are naturally strong and healthy, we should do our best to be as strong and healthy as we are able.

Our strength is given to us for God's purposes. Psalm 18 says, "He trains my hands for war, so that my arms can bend a bow of bronze" (v. 34).

We will be humbled by the reality of living in a fallen world, and our bodies will break, but we should cultivate them as best we can. We should be wise with what we put in our bodies. We should get as strong as we can so we can use our strength for others.

GROUP DISCUSSION QUESTIONS

1. How do you treat your body?

_____

_____

_____

_____

_____

2. Did God gift you with strength and health or do you have to fight for it?

_____

_____

_____

_____

3. What is your current plan for forging the vessel of your body?

_____

_____

_____

_____

4. How have you abused the vessel of your body in the past? What commitment will you make to the group to change these habits?

_____

_____

_____

_____

5. Why does it matter that we are strong and healthy?

_____

_____

_____

_____

PRAYER

Have one man volunteer to pray over the topic of forging the vessel of the body. Have him pray for the group and ask for direction from God. You can use the following prayer if it's helpful:

> _Father, you gave us our bodies. As men, you made us to be useful._
> _You gave some of us physical strength. We confess that all too_

often we have misused our bodies. We have been poor stewards. Would you guide us in the way of health and strength? Would you remind us that health and strength aren't everything, and that they are in fact nothing if they become an idol? Build us, God. Make our hands strong for battle. In Jesus's name, amen.

TAKE ACTION

It's time to forge your vessel. Not on Monday, not next week, but today. Consider what action you will take to make your body stronger and healthier starting today. Do you need to improve your nutrition? Take up a new exercise regimen? Do something and do it immediately, even if you don't have a grand plan. Consider it a permanent lifestyle change toward forging your vessel. You may adjust your plan over time, but remain committed to forging the vessel of your body.

CHAPTER 8

Ignite the Heart

FLY-BY OVERVIEW

A man is driven by the affections of his heart, and a full-hearted man lives a meaningful life. During boyhood, our hearts are ablaze. We run, play, and laugh. But as we grow up, the embers in our chests cool. How do we get them back? Getting outdoors will certainly help to stir our affections for God—especially in majestic places. Art helps, too, and men should not only consume art—they should produce it. A man should also be present where he is. He should, with an engaged heart and mind, be in the moment. Our boyhood hearts are not gone, but we must do some work to get them back.

GROUP DISCUSSION QUESTIONS

1. How is your heart? What do you long for?

   _____

   _____

   _____

   _____

   _____

2. What is your life like when you live full-hearted?

_____

_____

_____

_____

_____

3. When is the last time nature terrified you? When is the last time you spent time in nature?

_____

_____

_____

_____

_____

4. Do you value art? Why should you?

_____

_____

_____

_____

_____

5. Do you want that boyish joy back? Maybe your childhood wasn't joyful, but do you remember the awe you had for life? How will you take yourself less seriously today and start to enjoy life again like a boy?

_____

_____

_____

_____

_____

PRAYER

Have one man volunteer to pray over the hearts of the men in your Storm Group. Have him pray for the group and ask for direction from God. You can use the following prayer if it's helpful:

> *God, we want our hearts back. We have allowed them to grow cold in certain places, and this will not do. We want to live under your kingship with joy and passion. Help us rekindle our hearts around Jesus, and may our lives be set ablaze by his transformation. Amen.*

TAKE ACTION

This week you will work on your heart. Specifically, you will work on stirring your awe of God. This will stoke the embers in your heart. What you choose to do this week will vary based upon your tastes and environment. Here are some options:

1. Go camping

2. Write a poem or short story

3. Go to a great concert

4. Paint something

5. Make a great meal for a loved one

CHAPTER 9

The Gentleman Savage

FLY-BY OVERVIEW

Jesus is the lion and the lamb. He is the perfect balance of ferocity and tenderness. As men, we should seek to be the same. We should seek to be Gentleman Savages. When a man knows he is physically capable, he doesn't have to go around picking fights. He can choose to be a man of peace, and he is able to step up and defend the defenseless if need be. The Gentleman Savage should have dignity and respect for others. He should season his speech. He should be ready to put his physicality to use (if he is able) out of love for others.

GROUP DISCUSSION QUESTIONS

1. What does a Gentleman Savage look like to you?

2. How did Jesus display his lion attributes?

_____

_____

_____

_____

3. How did Jesus display his lamb attributes?

_____

_____

_____

_____

4. Why does it matter that a man test his body?

_____

_____

_____

_____

5. Do you have seasoned speech? What does your choice of language say to others about Jesus?

_____

_____

_____

_____

PRAYER

Have one man volunteer to pray. Have him pray for the group and ask for direction from God. You can use the following prayer if it's helpful:

> *Jesus, you are the lion and the lamb. You are ferocious and you are tender. We confess that too often we've been either too ferocious or too tender. Lord, it's not just that we want to be like you—though we do. But we want to be with you and to know you more. Help us know you more, and in doing so help us balance our inner lion and lamb. In your ferocious yet tender name, amen.*

TAKE ACTION

This week will be a week to cultivate peace in your life. Sure, trying martial arts would be one good application of this chapter, and if you are so inclined, I say go for it. But I think we need to start with peace. Is there any unresolved conflict in your life? What opportunities do you have to make peace in your world?

Remember the words of Romans 12:18: "If possible, so far as it depends on you, live peaceably with all."

This verse contemplates the difficulty of making peace with violent people, people who'd rather cultivate strife than peace. But do you see it? "So far as it depends on you…" Do what you can this week to seek forgiveness and to give it to others.

CHAPTER 10

Building Disruption

FLY-BY OVERVIEW

The Christian man should be disruptive in a good way. He should live weirdly because of the power of the love inside of him. Jesus imparts this love to his followers by way of his Spirit, and once we are drenched in the love of Christ we cannot help but live differently. If our hearts are captivated by Jesus we will love scandalously and seek to build disruptive organizations. We will, because of Jesus's work in us, disrupt the world.

GROUP DISCUSSION QUESTIONS

1. Are you currently living disruptively?

2. Picture the godly men you know. What is weird about them? How are they different from non-believing men?

_____

_____

_____

_____

_____

3. Do you speak up to share the truth of the gospel with others?

_____

_____

_____

_____

_____

4. What are some disruptive organizations that magnify the glory of Christ?

_____

_____

_____

_____

5. What are some ways you can make a ruckus in your life to love others and glorify God?

_____

_____

_____

_____

PRAYER

Have one man volunteer to pray over the topic of disruptive living. Have him pray for the group and ask for direction from God. You can use the following prayer if it's helpful:

> *Lord, you are the Creator of this world. You gave us the free will to sin, and we did. We do. And thus this world is broken because of us. But we know you are telling us a great love story. We know you are disrupting this world with your grace. Help us be men who disrupt our environments with that same love. Show us how to make a ruckus for your name's sake. Amen.*

TAKE ACTION

What risk do you need to take this week? Do you need to go ahead and start that business or that book? Do you need to engage someone in your life with the love of Christ—a love so foreign it disrupts them? Take one disruptively loving action this week.

CHAPTER 11

Endure

FLY-BY OVERVIEW

A manly life is a tiring life. A man should be tired. At the end of each day, we should be wrung out. We need to rest in the Lord and recharge to keep us going. We should be kind to ourselves, but we should also learn to man up and push on. We are trucks, not sports cars. We should be careful that we aren't taken out, as Satan would love to pick us off. Jesus offers his rest and energy if we will commune with him. He is The Well.

GROUP DISCUSSION QUESTIONS

1. Are you tired?

2. How do you find physical rest? What about spiritual rest? Which is more important to you?

3. What about Douglas Mawson's story inspires you?

    _____

    _____

    _____

    _____

4. How might you cultivate your toughness?

    _____

    _____

    _____

    _____

5. Jesus is the source of all deep rest. Have each man explain to the group how he will, starting today, make sure he rests in God.

    _____

    _____

    _____

    _____

PRAYER

Have one man volunteer to pray over the issue of endurance. Have him pray for the group and ask for direction from God. You can use the following prayer if it's helpful:

> _Lord, we're weary. This life is hard. But it's nothing you don't understand. You tread our paths. You know our pains. You are a sympathetic and loving God. We want to endure to the end. We want to run the race well as faithful men. Give us your spiritual nourishment and guide us as to where we should go. Amen._

TAKE ACTION

Consider how, if you were your enemy, you would destroy yourself. What tactics would you employ? How would you distract yourself, and what would be the plan of attack? "The devil prowls around like a roaring lion, seeking someone to devour" (1 Peter 5:8). This week, take action to fortify your defenses. Ask God to protect you, and look around your life to see where you're vulnerable. Are you at risk of adultery or lust? Are you at risk of drinking yourself into destruction? Maybe you're just tired and need some rest. Fortify your defenses this week, and as you do so, keep a long-term perspective. You are preparing yourself to endure.

CHAPTER 12

Die Hard

FLY-BY OVERVIEW

Death is coming. It spares no one. But for the Christian, death is merely a transition. We need to get over our fear of death so we can get busy living. If we will cultivate our deathbed perspective, we will live fuller lives. As men living under the kingship of Jesus, we are never done. We need older men to keep running the race. If we walk in God's ways, we will build a legacy. We will tell a story with our lives that will help the men who go after us to see what to do and what not to do. We will, God willing, tell the story of our King.

GROUP DISCUSSION QUESTIONS

1. When is the first time you experienced the death of a loved one? How did it affect you?

_____

_____

_____

_____

_____

2. Are you afraid to die?

_____

_____

_____

3. How does deathbed perspective help you live a meaningful life?

_____

_____

_____

4. Why do we need older men to keep running hard?

_____

_____

_____

5. What story will your life tell those who come after you? What story do you want to tell?

_____

_____

_____

_____

_____

PRAYER

Have one man volunteer to pray over the legacies of the men in the Storm Group. Have him pray for the group and ask for direction from God. You can use the following prayer if it's helpful:

Father, we want to leave a legacy. It's not that we just want to pack the chapel for our funeral, but rather we want those who come after us to see your hand guiding our lives. We know when we die we come to you, so we are not scared. Help us live boldly, fearlessly. Help us show ourselves as men. Amen.

TAKE ACTION

Imagine you are in a hospital bed on the verge of death. The doctor has given you one day to live and you know that soon you'll slip away. You look back on your life and consider what really mattered and what didn't. Take some time to write down what you think will matter and what won't—and then adjust your life accordingly. Write it below:

WHAT MATTERS   **WHAT DOESN'T MATTER**

A Final Word

I hope this study was useful to you. I hope it challenged you and encouraged you. There is nothing greater for this world than for men to be men. Specifically, there is nothing greater for this world than for men to live whole lives under the kingship of Jesus.

We need you.

Your life is not an accident. God has you here on this earth to do something. You have a field to cultivate and a battle to fight. Rise up and meet your adventure with God.

The greatest prize of life is intimacy with Jesus. You see, when David told Solomon to show himself a man, he was not talking about putting on appearances. David knew if Solomon would walk in the ways of God, he would grow in his intimacy with him. Because of God's work in him, Solomon's life would tell a story which would reveal who he really was. David and Solomon were men in the royal family of God. And so are you.

After completing this study, do not go back to your old way of living. Draw closer to Jesus. Let him kill your fears and inspire you to action. Get out there, and show yourself a man.

Checking In

In an effort to reinforce the progress you made during your Storm Group, you should do a check-in one year after the last group meeting. The group leader should try to get the group back together in person, but if this is not possible he should at least have everyone communicate via email or phone call.

Write down your answers to the following questions. Be as honest as possible.

1. What idols has God slayed over the past year?

   _____

   _____

   _____

2. Do you remember your identity as an adopted son of God on a daily basis? What would help remind you?

   _____

   _____

   _____

3. How have you expanded your mind this year?

   _____

   _____

   _____

4. Have you worked to forge the vessel of your body this year? What progress, if any, have you made?

_____

_____

5. How is your heart? Have you pursued worship of God in nature?

_____

_____

6. How often do you read God's Word?

_____

_____

7. What is God teaching you?

_____

_____

8. Did you read the book you committed to read?

_____

_____

9. Are there any unconfessed sins in your life that you need to confess to your brothers? (You do not have to write this down, but you should confess them if need be.)

_____

_____

10. What areas of your life need to be submitted to God for his grace, power, and healing?

_____

_____

Don't be too hard on yourself. We all need the grace of Christ. This assessment is not a test, but rather a tool of awareness. Let your answers remind you of your need for Jesus. The dominant force of your life is that which you worship, so turn your worship where it belongs: to Jesus. As you do so, he will make you more like him.

www.ingramcontent.com/pod-product-compliance
Lightning Source LLC
Chambersburg PA
CBHW061843040426
42447CB00012B/3110